YOU'VE GOT IT MADE

ALSO BY MARIAN BURROS

Keep It Simple: 30-Minute Meals from Scratch

Pure & Simple: Delicious Recipes for Additive-Free Cooking

Elegant but Easy

Freeze with Ease

Come for Cocktails, Stay for Supper

The Summertime Cookbook